Kindness
is my Superpower

POSITIVE AFFIRMATIONS & ACTIONS FOR
IMPROVING YOUR SELF-WORTH, HAPPINESS,
EMPATHY, GRATITUDE & SELF-LOVE

🐢Turtle Publishing

Published by Turtle Publishing
All rights reserved.

Printed on demand in Australia, United States and United Kingdom.

Written & designed by Kathy Shanks
© Kathy Shanks 2021
Illustrations by Freepik Storyset & Turtle Publishing

No part of this publication may be reproduced, stored in a retrieval system, or transmitted in any form or by any means, electronic, mechanical, photocopying, recording or otherwise, without the prior written permission of the author.

Under no circumstances will any blame or legal responsibility be held against the publisher, or author, for any damages, reparation, or monetary loss due to the information contained within this book including, but not limited to — errors, omissions, or inaccuracies. Either directly or indirectly. You are responsible for your own choices, actions, and results.

Legal Notice: This book is copyright protected. This book is only for personal use. You cannot amend, distribute, sell, use, quote or paraphrase any part, or the content within this book, without the consent of the author or publisher.

Disclaimer: Please note the information contained within this document is for educational and entertainment purposes only. All effort has been executed to present accurate, up to date, and reliable, complete information. No warranties of any kind are declared or implied. Readers acknowledge that the author is not engaging in the rendering of legal, financial, medical or professional advice. The content within this book has been derived from various sources. Please consult a licensed professional before attempting any techniques outlined in this book.

SPECIAL BONUS
FREE BOOKS

FREE Workbook to begin an intentional journaling practice.

FREE 30 Days to Greater Self Love Program

Get FREE unlimited access to these AND all of my new books by joining our fan base!

SCAN WITH YOUR CAMERA OR GO TO
bit.ly/AffGifts

How to use this book

On the left-hand pages are affirmations. On the right-hand pages are actions for you to take towards strengthening your kind heart.

You may like to work through this book one page per day, or perhaps you'd like to trust divine guidance. Hold this book close to your heart or navel, close your eyes, take three gentle breaths, and as you breathe out on the third breath, open the book. We trust that you will be guided to the page you need the most.

Introduction

Imagine if every single person treated each other with empathy, generosity, and compassion. Imagine if judgment, prejudice, or discrimination simply didn't exist. Imagine a world where kindness is so commonplace that it's the norm. Wouldn't that be exactly the kind of world you'd want to live in?

But, let's face it: the fact is, it isn't always easy to be kind.

Most of the time, we simply forget to be kind—it's not like we go out of our way to be awful to other people. Chances are, we're not even unkind, exactly, just… disengaged. We're just so preoccupied with working hard to make sure our own (or our families') needs are met that we can't even begin to think of extending ourselves to others.

Often, being in a constant rush to take care of the many things on our plates can also be overwhelming and stressful. Sometimes, this can lead to less-than-ideal choices regarding how we deal with those around us. You know those instances—those moments when you pick a fight with your partner or snap at your toddler over the littlest of things at the end of a long, exhausting day.

Perhaps worse than being too busy for kindness is how we've become jaded and cynical. With time, the realities of the world have made us hard—we know all about the negativity and darkness that's undeniably out there. We see it on the news, or sometimes firsthand, around us, and sadly, it all has taught us to do everything we can to protect ourselves. Being kind comes with a certain vulnerability that can be hard to open ourselves up to.

There's also no denying that it can be difficult sometimes to see our differences through the lens of understanding. Whatever these differences may be—whether in how we think or act, what we look like or believe—kindness can often require us to put ourselves in each other's shoes. That is definitely no easy feat.

So, we all want a kinder world, but it can sometimes feel impossible to achieve. Not only is putting it in motion a challenge, but you might even find yourself thinking, "I'm just one person, after all. What difference could I possibly make?"

Well, to put it in perspective: have you ever been on the receiving end of someone else's kindness, especially on a particularly bad day? Maybe a co-worker randomly complimented your hair at a time when you didn't feel the least bit attractive. Or, perhaps a stranger held the elevator door for you and saved you from being late to a meeting. It cost them no more than 15 seconds, and they probably did it without thinking… and yet it made all the difference to you, right? You can never know what others are going through—don't underestimate the impact you're capable of making in other people's lives. And, perhaps more importantly, the ripples you can put in motion.

The thing about kindness is that it doesn't have to be big. Being kind doesn't have to mean donating all your money to charity or dedicating your life to volunteering. The truth is, it very rarely takes the form of a grand gesture.

In fact, one of the most effective forms of kindness is being kind to yourself. To even begin to share yourself—your time, resources, talents—with others, you first have to fill your own cup. This only comes with consistently treating yourself with respect and love.

Whether towards yourself or others, practising kindness is all about starting small and doing things with intention. While it can sometimes be easy to confuse being nice with being kind, the two aren't the same—you can lend a helping hand while being resentful about it. Kindness goes beyond behaviour. It entails cultivating a spirit of generosity, empathy, and compassion.

Because kindness starts from within before radiating outwards, affirmations can be powerful tools to kindle this spirit.

Our brains are wired to 'take note of' patterns of thinking we consistently use and 'remember' these for easy access later on. The more we repeat certain things in our minds, the more natural it becomes for us to harness these later on.

Whether you choose to say them out loud, write them down in a journal, or just focus on them mentally, regularly repeating these short statements can help you focus your energy on positivity. A regular affirmation practice can help you re-centre on the essential values you hold in your heart and know to be true.

Of course, kindness must eventually find its way out into the world in the form of action. Again, remember that even the smallest, simplest things can make a huge difference, as long as they are done mindfully and with heart.

Kindness can change the world… and it all starts within each of us.

"Be kind to others, so that you may learn the secret art of being kind to yourself."

- Paramahansa Yogananda

AFFIRMATIONS

I am generous
with my gifts
and use these
to lift others up.

ACTIONS

Make it a point to consciously do at least one selfless thing each and every day. It doesn't matter if it's big or small, as long as it is done with heartfelt intention.

AFFIRMATIONS

I treat
others with
compassion.

ACTIONS

Compliment people freely, genuinely, and often.

AFFIRMATIONS

I am always willing to lend a helping hand to those who need it.

ACTIONS

Host a nice dinner or get together for some of your closest friends.

AFFIRMATIONS

I am a loving,
giving person.

ACTIONS

Send a sincere message of support to someone you think might be in need of it.

AFFIRMATIONS

Being able to positively impact someone else makes me happy.

ACTIONS

Write about an instance someone was kind to you—the positive impact they had on your life or even just on your day, how it made you feel, and what you learned from it.

AFFIRMATIONS

I love seeing others succeed.

ACTIONS

Brighten up a co-worker's morning by surprising them with coffee.

AFFIRMATIONS

I am happy to celebrate my loved ones' triumphs right along with them.

ACTIONS

If you're qualified and able, donate blood.

AFFIRMATIONS

I am sensitive to the needs of others.

ACTIONS

Leave little sticky notes with messages of encouragement or uplifting quotes where strangers might unexpectedly find them.

AFFIRMATIONS

I am excited to inspire and empower those around me.

ACTIONS

Support small local businesses—trying out their offerings and spreading the word go a long way.

AFFIRMATIONS

I am a safe space for those who need it.

ACTIONS

Volunteer at your local animal shelter.

AFFIRMATIONS

Giving brings me joy.

ACTIONS

Clean out your closet and donate items that are still in good shape to a homeless shelter or local charity.

AFFIRMATIONS

I am a source of joy and positivity for others.

ACTIONS

Along with (or even instead of) traditional presents, make meaningful donations to chosen charities in your loved ones' names for their birthdays.

AFFIRMATIONS

I am mindful of speaking from a place of positivity.

ACTIONS

Write about an act of kindness you witnessed recently.

AFFIRMATIONS

My heart is gracious and forgiving.

ACTIONS

Hand out cold beverages to your mailmen, garbage collectors, or delivery persons on hot days.

AFFIRMATIONS

I treat everyone equally, regardless of our wonderful differences.

ACTIONS

Visit an aged care home and just spend time hanging out and chatting with an elderly person in need of a friend.

I am kind not only in my actions but also in my thoughts and words.

ACTIONS

'Adopt' or sponsor wildlife online or make a donation to an ecological conservation project.

AFFIRMATIONS

I am a thoughtful friend.

ACTIONS

Phone a friend you haven't talked to in a while just to check in on them and catch up.

AFFIRMATIONS

I find joy in bringing out the best in other people.

ACTIONS

Hug a family member or friend when they need it the most.

AFFIRMATIONS

I am happy when I can make someone else smile.

ACTIONS

Be someone's sounding board or even shoulder to cry on.

AFFIRMATIONS

I treat every single person around me with respect.

ACTIONS

Read a child their favourite book.

AFFIRMATIONS

I always listen genuinely and try to keep an open mind, even with beliefs or opinions that are different from mine.

ACTIONS

Practice noticing those around you who are struggling or having a rough time. You might not always be in a position to help them, but extending a little empathy and extra patience goes a long way.

AFFIRMATIONS

When I give, I do it freely and wholeheartedly.

ACTIONS

Bring over a meal to share with a friend or family member who lives alone.

AFFIRMATIONS

I put my heart into helping others.

ACTIONS

Hold the door or elevator for someone.

AFFIRMATIONS

I am a good listener.

ACTIONS

Carve out at least 10 minutes each day just to show yourself some love in whatever way you choose.

AFFIRMATIONS

I am 100% present when I am with people I care about.

ACTIONS

Offer to babysit for a friend or relative.

AFFIRMATIONS

I am love embodied.

ACTIONS

Spread positivity online—repost, reblog, or share things that made you smile!

AFFIRMATIONS

I fill my cup so I can keep being a blessing to others.

ACTIONS

Buy someone flowers… just because.

AFFIRMATIONS

I fuel my actions
with love.

ACTIONS

Is there someone in your life you owe an apology to? Write a heartfelt letter to give them whenever you're ready.

AFFIRMATIONS

I truly enjoy setting others up for success.

ACTIONS

Share your skills or knowledge with someone without asking for anything in return. It could be anything from simply answering a co-worker's question to the best of your abilities, to helping a neighbour out with a home improvement project.

AFFIRMATIONS

I am a light
in someone's
darkness.

ACTIONS

Let someone else take over the playlist during a long drive.

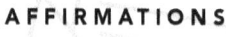

AFFIRMATIONS

I speak up and stand against injustice.

ACTIONS

Surprise your partner with an amazing breakfast in bed.

AFFIRMATIONS

I move from
a place of
empathy and
understanding.

ACTIONS

Every time you buy a new non-necessity for yourself, donate an old belonging—anything, really—to someone in need.

AFFIRMATIONS

I genuinely enjoy lending a helping hand.

ACTIONS

Greet waiters, retail staff, and other customer service workers with a sincere smile.

I am supportive, uplifting, and motivating.

ACTIONS

If you know someone who's moving house or doing some major home renovations, offer to help out.

AFFIRMATIONS

I refuse to speak ill of others behind their backs.

ACTIONS

Participate in a community cleanup activity or neighbourhood recycling drive.

AFFIRMATIONS

I am patient and considerate.

ACTIONS

Challenge yourself to compliment a stranger!

AFFIRMATIONS

I am filled with boundless
love for those around me.

ACTIONS

Happy with the service you received at a shop or restaurant? Take note of your server or attendant's name and put in a good word for them with their manager.

AFFIRMATIONS

I refuse to let fear get in the way of love and kindness.

ACTIONS

When a conversation you're in starts to veer towards gossip or negativity, try your best to turn it around or change the topic.

AFFIRMATIONS

I live life with an open, ever-expanding heart.

ACTIONS

Always remember your pleases and thank yous.

AFFIRMATIONS

I am proud of the positivity I put out into the world.

ACTIONS

Sign up to be an official organ donor.

AFFIRMATIONS

I radiate love
and goodness.

ACTIONS

Learn about another culture—if you have a friend or colleague who belongs to that culture who's willing to share, even better!

AFFIRMATIONS

By allowing myself to be led by love, I cannot fail.

ACTIONS

Comment on friends' social media posts with sincere compliments and uplifting words.

AFFIRMATIONS

I am always ready to stand strong for those who cannot.

ACTIONS

Send a couple of friends some handwritten snail mail. Better yet, surprise them with some lovely postcards even if you're from the same city!

AFFIRMATIONS

I have so much to give and share.

ACTIONS

Don't be afraid to get vocal about causes you are passionate about.

AFFIRMATIONS

Every life
is equally,
tremendously
precious.

ACTIONS

Do your best to talk about ideas, not people.

I am kind
without
condition.

ACTIONS

Remember that confrontation doesn't necessarily have to be a negative thing. In situations where you need to call someone out, check yourself and make sure you are coming from a place of love and a genuine desire to uplift others.

AFFIRMATIONS

I am so blessed
to be able
to share with
others.

ACTIONS

Leave little notes of love and affection around the house for your partner to find unexpectedly.

AFFIRMATIONS

My capacity for loving others is limitless.

ACTIONS

If someone asks you a question you don't readily know the answer to, take the time to look it up and get back to them.

AFFIRMATIONS

I am happy to set the stage for others to shine.

ACTIONS

Make something for someone. It can be anything (a poem or song, handmade jewellery, a batch of cookies… anything), as long as you made it yourself and put your heart into it.

AFFIRMATIONS

I let go of all my negative biases and preconceived notions of others.

ACTIONS

Ask a loved one about their goals. How can you support their journey in your own little way? What can you do to help them achieve those goals?

AFFIRMATIONS

I value and cherish the trust others put in me.

ACTIONS

If you have kids (or any children in your life), encourage them to donate their old toys and books.

AFFIRMATIONS

Each person on this earth is uniquely beautiful and unique.

ACTIONS

Sign petitions for causes you care about.

AFFIRMATIONS

I cultivate peace
in any way I can.

ACTIONS

Hand over the remote control to someone else and let them have free reign over family TV time.

AFFIRMATIONS

Kindness is what makes the world a beautiful place.

ACTIONS

Sign up for a charity run.

AFFIRMATIONS

I accept others just as they are.

ACTIONS

Put 'stray' groceries back where they belong as often as you can when you spot them at the store.

AFFIRMATIONS

I am my best
self when I help
others.

ACTIONS

Pack an extra snack or lunch to take to the office and share with a co-worker.

AFFIRMATIONS

I always try to see where someone is coming from.

ACTIONS

Tape a bit of change to a random vending machine.

AFFIRMATIONS

I approach conflict with compassion.

ACTIONS

Stop for a talented busker or street performer. Don't forget to give them a generous donation afterwards.

AFFIRMATIONS

I have the
power to
change
someone's life
for the better.

ACTIONS

Share your favourite recipe with someone who loves to cook.

AFFIRMATIONS

My gentleness is my strength.

ACTIONS

Try out eco-friendly, sustainable swaps for some everyday items such as straws and single-use plastic containers.

AFFIRMATIONS

I accept that sometimes, kindness means saying 'no'.

ACTIONS

Leave some change at the laundromat for strangers.

AFFIRMATIONS

I let go of any grudges or past conflicts.

ACTIONS

Go out of your way to make a new friend.

AFFIRMATIONS

Each day
holds endless
opportunities to
be kind.

ACTIONS

Pick up extra chores around the house without being asked.

AFFIRMATIONS

I am grateful for the things I can share.

ACTIONS

Set up a bird or butterfly feeder right outside your house.

AFFIRMATIONS

Kindness comes to me effortlessly and without burden.

ACTIONS

Make someone laugh (or at least crack a smile) every day.

AFFIRMATIONS

I advocate for the weak and less fortunate.

ACTIONS

If allowed, bring a couple of balloons to your local children's hospital.

I choose to
be loving in
the face of
adversity.

ACTIONS

Whenever you spot a kid's lemonade stand (or any other similar young entrepreneur's venture), make a purchase.

AFFIRMATIONS

I am
emboldened
by a soul that's
loving and kind.

ACTIONS

Pick up litter in your neighbourhood park.

AFFIRMATIONS

I hold kindness
above all else.

ACTIONS

For any and all appointments, make it a habit to show up on time, every time.

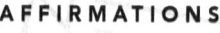

AFFIRMATIONS

I never give up on the people I love.

ACTIONS

Know someone who's planning a holiday? Offer to help them get organised and stay on top of everything.

AFFIRMATIONS

I extend my help mindfully and with sensitivity.

ACTIONS

Never stop trying to be a better human being—make a list of 'kindness resolutions.' How can you be a more supportive friend? A more loving partner? A dream teammate?

AFFIRMATIONS

I am building a kinder world.

ACTIONS

Leave small plush toys or old tennis balls at a dog park.

AFFIRMATIONS

I honour people's differences and what makes them unique.

ACTIONS

Offer your seat to someone else on public transport.

AFFIRMATIONS

There is never anything to be lost in giving.

ACTIONS

Celebrate your friends' milestones! Whether it's a wedding, a showcase for a hobby they're passionate about, a dog adoption day... if it's important to them, be sure to show your unwavering support.

AFFIRMATIONS

I refuse to judge others and put people down.

ACTIONS

Do a random act of kindness for someone, and challenge them to pay it forward in whatever way they can.

Also available by **Kathy Shanks**...

Guided Journaling is available worldwide as print or ebook at Amazon, Booktopia, Barnes & Noble and all good bookstores.

Also available in Australia from **turtlepublishing.com.au**

Inside this book you'll discover how to use my method of journaling to:

- Work towards creating balance for heart, mind, body and soul without sacrificing career and relationships
- Create rituals that help you develop gratitude
- Use daily affirmations to practice positivity and manifest your future dreams
- Discover strategies to improve your relationships, build your life mission, start a side hustle, discover yourself, develop self-love, improve your health AND improve your mindset

It seems too good to be true, right! Organising your thoughts and dreams in 10-20 minutes a day can be that one simple change that actually makes your dreams become a reality.

Make your journal your safe haven, a place of nurturing for you to come and reflect, clear your mind, set goals, develop gratitude, make plans, dream, and take steps towards the future that has always seemed just out of reach.

Please join our journaling community at
facebook.com/groups/kathyshanks
for exclusive insider access to updates and releases

Also available in the
Guided Journaling Series...

Journaling for a
Balanced Life with a
Health focus

Journaling for a
Balanced Life with a
Life Mission focus

Journaling for a
Balanced Life with a
focus on the **Heart**

Journaling for a
Balanced Life with a
Gratitude & **Manifest** focus

We have a selection of *journals* available worldwide as
print or ebook at Amazon, Booktopia,
Barnes & Noble and all good bookstores.
Also available in Australia from **turtlepublishing.com.au**

www.ingramcontent.com/pod-product-compliance
Lightning Source LLC
Chambersburg PA
CBHW020323010526
44107CB00054B/1958